My Scrapbook

Julie

_____
Name

7

_____
Age

Today I can smell spring.
There are flowers everywhere.

My tulips

2

My street

My garden

3

Grandpa sent me some photos from the farm. Hurry up, summer!

Dear Julie,

There are lots of new things for you to see. We have our first lamb. It is called a Jacob sheep. Jess has a new foal, and there will be a surprise when you get here.

Love,
Grandpa

Jacob sheep

My cousin, Sara

Grandma's peach trees
in full bloom

5

Summer is the **BEST!**
I love it at the farm.
Jess and her foal, Dolly,
are the greatest.

Grandpa's surprise
was two puppies!
One is for me.
I call him Sam.
The other one is Benny.

Sam
and
Benny

Lavender

Jess
and Dolly

7

Our town is

hot, hot, hot!

I am taking swimming lessons.

Mum and Billy love Sam, too.

Swimming lessons

8

Billy in the garden

Me picking
flowers

9

The leaves are changing.
Autumn is here.

Mum and I went
apple picking.

Leaves

We picked
a lot of apples.

Autumn leaves

We ate six apples.

We went to the park.
We saw a squirrel
hiding nuts. I wish
I had my own camera!

Dear Julie,

Grandma and I went to the lake.
It was beautiful.

We are making hay now.
Dolly is growing fast.

Hope you like the photos
of Grandma!

Miss you,
Grandpa

Tansies

Squirrel hiding nuts

Duck

Goose

Grandma's birds

Chicken

Guinea hen

It is dark early now.
We made a bird feeder
for our garden.

Dear Julie,

Winter is here. The ponies have long, shaggy coats so they can stay warm. Uncle Jeff, Grandpa, and I are staying busy feeding the animals. We hope you like your birthday present.

Happy Birthday!

Love,
Grandma

Pony

14

Uncle Jeff feeding the pigs

Twigs

Bird feeder

Today is my birthday.
Grandma and Grandpa
sent me a camera!

My first picture

16